Teens and Gender Dysphoria

Don Nardo

ReferencePoint
Press®

San Diego, CA

© 2017 ReferencePoint Press, Inc.
Printed in the United States

For more information, contact:
ReferencePoint Press, Inc.
PO Box 27779
San Diego, CA 92198
www.ReferencePointPress.com

LIBRARY OF CONGRESS CATALOGING-IN-PUBLICATION DATA

Names: Nardo, Don, 1947- author.
Title: Teens and gender dysphoria / by Don Nardo.
Description: San Diego, CA : ReferencePoint Press, Inc., 2017. | Series: Teen mental health series | Audience: Grade 9 to 12. | Includes bibliographical references and index.
Identifiers: LCCN 2016035290 (print) | LCCN 2016035776 (ebook) | ISBN 9781682821244 (hardback) | ISBN 9781682821251 (eBook)
Subjects: LCSH: Gender identity disorders in children--Juvenile literature. | Gender identity disorders in adolescence--Juvenile literature.
Classification: LCC RJ506.G35 N37 2017 (print) | LCC RJ506.G35 (ebook) | DDC 618.92/8583--dc23
LC record available at https://lccn.loc.gov/2016035290

CONTENTS

"God Made a Mistake"

Brandon Simms was born in the year 2000 in a tiny Southern town. In his first few years of life, he said and did things that at first amused and later worried his parents. For example, his mother, Tina, remembers how she and her husband, Bill, laughed heartily when, in a local Italian restaurant, the two-year-old said his first full sentence. "I like your high heels," the boy informed a nearby woman wearing a red dress.[1]

Also, Tina recalls, at age two and three Brandon often expressed a serious dislike for his boy's clothes. At times he would pull them off and insist that his mother let him wear underclothes and shoes from her closet. Thinking these requests to be cute and harmless, Tina sometimes let her son don these items. "He ruined all my heels in the sandbox," she says with a smile.[2]

A Phase That Never Passed

Tina was a bit concerned, however, one day when she was giving Brandon, still three, a bath. At one point he climbed out of the tub, tucked his penis between his legs, and started dancing in front of the mirror. "Look, Mom," he crowed happily. "I'm a girl!"[3]

These sorts of incidents continued to occur regularly for the next two years. Eventually, more than a little worried, Tina had a serious talk with her son. Calmly but firmly, she said, "Brandon, God made you a boy for a special reason." Before she could continue with her carefully prepared speech, Brandon blurted out, "God made a mistake!"[4]

Tina took Brandon to several therapists. The first one said the boy was just going through a phase, but Tina subsequently observed that the so-called phase never passed. Then, out of the blue, Tina's mother, in whom she had confided about Brandon's seemingly strange antics, arrived at the family home. The boy's grandmother eagerly showed Tina a Barbara Walters *20/20* special she had recorded. The program showed a six-year-old boy named "Jazz." Since he was a toddler, he had enjoyed dressing like a girl. In fact, everything young Jazz had done to reject his maleness and embrace a feminine identity was completely familiar to Tina. Walters mentioned the name of the condition the two boys clearly exhibited — "gender identity disorder." Medical experts, Walters went on, call those who have that condition "transgender."[5]

A Stunning Realization

Like millions of Americans at the time, Tina and Bill had never heard the term *transgender*. They had long assumed that Brandon's displays of apparent gender confusion were unique to him alone. Once she had viewed the Barbara Walters program, however, Tina hurried to the nearest computer and Googled the words *transgender children*. That quickly educated her about the condition; it also led her to a subculture of parents of transgender children living all across the country. These mothers

> "This is nothing we can fix. In his brain, in his *mind*, Brandon's a girl."[6]
>
> —Tina, Brandon's mother

and fathers shared their own similar experiences with both little boys and little girls who consistently rejected the gender indicated by their own bodies.

Eventually, just as those parents, along with medical experts, had already concluded, Tina came to what was for her a stunning realization. "This is nothing we can fix," she says of Brandon's case. "In his brain, in his *mind*, Brandon's a girl." Echoing medical articles she had been reading, she continues, "It's just a medical condition, like diabetes or something." It is nothing to be ashamed of, she realized. It is "just a variation on human behavior."[6]

Transgender teen Jazz Jennings (left) appears with her mother in New York in 2015. Jennings, who was interviewed at age six on ABC's 20/20, has emerged as a leading advocate and role model for the transgender community.

Struggles with Who They Are

In these ways Brandon's parents came to an understanding of what it means to be transgender and proceeded to act in their child's best interests. They decided that his mental stability and happiness were more important than what people might think of his being a girl rather than a boy. In 2008, when the youngster was eight, they allowed him to assume a female identity. Brandon himself chose his new name—Bridget. In addition Tina took stacks of medical documentation with her to Bridget's school. Using this material as support, she educated the school officials on transgenderism and ensured that her child would be recognized as a girl and treated with respect.

A few years later, Tina and other parents of transgender children learned that medical authorities no longer considered simply being transgender a disorder. The experts dropped the label "gender identity disorder" and introduced a new term—"gender dysphoria." It turned out that Brandon's/Bridget's problem was not that he/she was transgender. Rather, for years the child had struggled with her gender identity, which sometimes made her unhappy.

Gender dysphoria became the official medical name of that struggle. Noted specialist in the condition, Dr. Johanna Olson, of Children's Hospital in Los Angeles, defines it as "persistent unhappiness, discomfort and distress about the incongruence [gap] between the gender that you are assigned, based on your anatomy at birth, versus the way you internally experience gender."[7]

That discomfort is what made Tina's son so strongly want to be accepted as the girl she was in her own mind. Thanks to young Brandon's loving, understanding parents, her dysphoria proved relatively mild. Once she identified as Bridget, she consistently felt happy.

However, across the country and throughout the world, many other transgender children have not been as fortunate. For one or more of a wide variety of reasons, some face serious struggles with who they are from a gender perspective. As Dr. Olson puts it, they often "experience difficult challenges from maybe their family, from their school, [or] from their church." All of those things, she says, "can present a whole scale of different problems for these kids."[8] Olson and other experts stress, however, that through education, understanding, and proper treatment, those problems can be solved.

> "[Gender dysphoria is] persistent unhappiness [about] the gender that you are assigned, based on your anatomy at birth, versus the way you internally experience gender."[7]
>
> —Gender identity specialist Dr. Johanna Olson

CHAPTER ONE

What Is Gender Dysphoria?

Gender dysphoria is a condition in which a person feels distress or discomfort about being transgender. Being transgender and suffering from gender dysphoria, however, are two different things, with very different definitions.

A Gap Between Biology and Feelings

A person is transgender when there is a disparity between his or her biological gender and the gender that his or her brain identifies with. One's biological gender is typically assigned at birth, based on the appearance of the infant's genitals. If the baby has a penis and testicles, the doctors designate him a boy. If the child has a vagina, the doctors pronounce her to be a girl.

As children grow older, from a mental and emotional standpoint, most of them comfortably identify with their biological gender. That is, biological males identify with, or feel like, boys. Similarly, biological females mentally and emotionally feel like girls.

However, in a small number of cases in each new generation, this mostly predictable situation does not hold true. In each of that small minority of cases, the person's mental and emotional gender identity does not match his or her assigned biological identity. In a very real sense, there is a gap between the physical biology that he or she was born with and his or her inward feelings. Such a person is said to be transgender.

Someone who is transgender therefore strongly feels that his or her inner self, so to speak, does not match up with the body he or she was born with. This is the origin of perhaps the most common complaint made by transgender people. It is either that "he" is trapped in the body of a female, or "she" is trapped in a male's body.

Seventeen-year-old Hunter Keith, for example, felt that he was a boy trapped in a female body. At the age of six, he told his mother, Roz, "I am a boy." She inquired whether or not he felt like he was a boy, and he answered, "I don't *feel* like a boy. I *am* a boy."[9]

According to Keith, when he was younger he was not yet familiar with the term *transgender*. At first all he knew was that he was a tomboy who intensely disliked wearing girl's clothes. When he went shopping for clothes with Roz, she found it curious that they always ended up in the boys' department. Roz also began to notice that her daughter seemed to be unusually preoccupied with photos of young boys with short haircuts.

> **"I don't *feel* like a boy. I *am* a boy."[9]**
>
> —Six-year-old Hunter Keith

As Keith himself explains, "I always knew something was up. I just didn't have the vocabulary to say 'I'm transgender.' I didn't have the knowledge that people could actually say, 'I'm a boy' if they weren't born with male parts." Thus, "once I found other people who felt the same way I did, then it made sense. But I never thought of it as a phase because I've always known who I was."[10]

Normal Deviations

Doctors who specialize in human sexuality have only recently come to understand what transgenderism is and how prevalent it is in society. They initially thought that simply being transgender was a mental disorder. Mental disorders are considered abnormal in the larger spectrum of human mental conditions. But the more cases of transgenderism that doctors uncovered, and the more they studied them in detail, the more they understood the condition's true nature.

Now the experts realize that transgender people are not abnormal. Rather, transgenderism is recognized as one of several mental conditions designated as "normal deviations" in the human

Social Acceptance Is Lowest
for Transgender People

Most LGBT individuals see little or no social acceptance of transgender people in society, according to a survey by the Pew Research Center. The survey results reveal their belief that all other groups in the LGBT community experience greater social acceptance than transgender individuals.

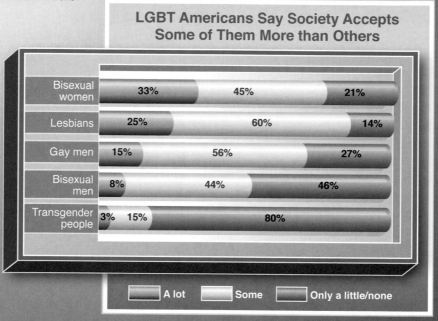

LGBT Americans Say Society Accepts Some of Them More than Others

	A lot	Some	Only a little/none
Bisexual women	33%	45%	21%
Lesbians	25%	60%	14%
Gay men	15%	56%	27%
Bisexual men	8%	44%	46%
Transgender people	3%	15%	80%

Source: Aleksandra Sandstrom, "Religious Groups' Policies on Transgender Members Vary Widely," Pew Research Center, December 2, 2015. www.pewresearch.org.

spectrum. A normal deviation is a condition that is quite normally shared by a minority of people in each new generation.

One of the more common examples is left-handedness. It has long been known that a majority of people in each generation are right-handed. The proportion of left-handed people in a given generation is always smaller than the proportion of right-handed people. At one time, before this phenomenon was well understood, many assumed that because left-handed individuals were in the minority, they were abnormal. As a result, in some societies parents and teachers forced left-handed people to write with their right hands so that they would be "normal." Eventually, however, scientists showed that although left-handedness is a deviation, it is a normal one. Thus, it is normal that a minority of people in each generation will be left-handed.

The same situation was found to hold true with several other minority conditions in the human spectrum. A minority of people have blue eyes, for instance, and they make up a group that is a normal deviation from the majority of people who have brown eyes. Still another example is homosexuality, or being gay. Experts now know that it is normal for a minority of people in each new generation to be gay. In a similar vein, people who are transgender make up still another group that is a normal deviation within the greater spectrum of human conditions.

How Many Americans Are Transgender?

Thus, it can be expected that any national, racial, or ethnic human group will consistently contain minorities of left-handed, blue-eyed, gay, and transgender people. The exact number of transgender people in American society is unknown, but various experts and organizations have made rough estimates. One of these organizations, the US Census Bureau, published a study on the topic in May 2015. It used data reported by citizens who had changed their gender identity and name with the Social Security Administration between 1936 and 2010. These reported changes numbered 135,367.

However, the coordinator of the study, Benjamin C. Harris, cautions that this was unlikely to be the exact number of transgender Americans in that period. "This approach," he admits, "surely misses certain transgender individuals." Those missing, he continues, include people who changed their names in court rather than through the Social Security Administration, "those who [did] not change their names at all, and those who [did] not have a Social Security number."[11]

Thus, the number of transgender Americans at any given moment in time is surely higher than the number cited in Harris's study. That was substantiated by a 2011 study put out by California's widely respected Williams Institute, which conducts research on sexual orientation. The study concluded that at least 700,000 adult

Why Knowing the Number of Transgender Americans Matters

In 2015 the Obama administration asked some federal agencies, including the Census Bureau, to find a credible way to learn how many Americans are transgender. Arizona representative Raúl M. Grijalva comments, "We need a much more comprehensive approach than we have right now." He points out that the Bureau of Justice Statistics already asks about gender identity in its National Inmate Survey. That study has found that transgender inmates experience unusually high rates of sexual assault while in prison. Also, in 2014, the FBI released statistics for hate crimes against transgender Americans.

These facts do not tell how large the US transgender population is, however. That number matters, says Samantha Michaels of *Mother Jones* magazine, because "without national demographic statistics policymakers may be fumbling in the dark when it comes to crafting legislation that helps trans people. And that's troubling, considering all the high-stakes questions" these lawmakers have recently had to consider. Among those questions is whether transgender children should be allowed to use school bathrooms that match up with their gender identity. The present lack of accurate data about gender identity in federal surveys "means we are ill-prepared to meet the needs of these communities," Rep. Grijalva states. "To go uncounted is to be unseen in the eyes of policymakers, which is why we must develop a credible and confidential understanding of these vulnerable populations we currently know too little about."

Samantha Michaels, "How Many Transgender Americans Are There?," *Mother Jones*, June 9, 2016. www
.motherjones.com.

Americans are transgender—about one in every 200 to 250 adults. Clearly, moreover, that estimate does not take into account the number of transgender children and teens, which remains unknown.

To Adjust or Not to Adjust

Whatever their overall numbers may be, some transgender people are able to adjust fairly well to the reality that their biological, or assigned, gender and their inner feelings do not match. Usually in such cases, the person is fortunate enough to find a lot of support from friends and family members. Hunter Keith was one of these lucky ones. He revealed his gender identity to some selected close friends first, even before telling his parents. He recalls, "It was more of a 'Let me run this by you. Maybe you can help me figure it out.' I was almost 100 percent sure they'd be okay with it, and every single one of my friends was completely supportive. They're still my best friends."[12]

Next Keith told his mother, Roz. Once she understood what he was talking about, she was fully supportive, as was his father. The young man proudly states,

> I don't think I'd be where I am without the people in my life. I know how much hate is out there and how many trans people struggle every day. As much as I'd like to be just a regular guy, I love the difference I'm making even more. My goal is to use my privilege to give people the same opportunities that I have.[13]

Not all transgender individuals have been as fortunate as Keith, as he himself points out. The everyday struggle he cites for many other "trans people," often includes various types of emotional upset and pain. Also frequent are feelings of rejection by family and friends who are not nearly as understanding as Keith's were. The combination of emotional upset, pain, and other discomforts that a transgender person may suffer while struggling with his or her gender identity is now known as gender dysphoria.

Typical of such suffering was that experienced by Michigan native Reid Ellefson-Frank. He had realized since age four that in his mind he was a boy, even though biologically he was born a girl. For years he suffered with this knowledge, feeling he could not tell anyone. "I was completely closeted," he says, "because I was afraid to be isolated and maybe face physical violence."[14]

> "I was completely closeted because I was afraid to be isolated and maybe face physical violence."[14]
>
> —Reid Ellefson-Frank

When he was a high school freshman, Ellefson-Frank finally told his parents and they accepted him for who he really was. But at school he was tormented and shunned. "People would challenge me a lot or just ignore me," he recalls. "I'd walk down the hall and hear them saying bad things behind my back. . . . I was amazed at how many opportunities closed to me. By mid-year, I knew I couldn't go back the next year."[15]

Certain Familiar Symptoms

Thus, one might see Hunter Keith's and Reid Ellefson-Frank's situations as two sides of the same coin. In this case, the coin itself consists of a person born with the biological, or assigned, physiology of a girl but the internal, mental outlook of a boy. On one side of that coin one finds Keith, who did not suffer significantly from gender dysphoria, and on the opposite side one finds Ellefson-Frank, who did.

The feelings these two young people had about themselves, and their individual outlooks on life, were clearly different. Experts say that that was to be expected. After all, gender dysphoria is an emotional condition characterized by certain symptoms, or outward signs. Just as a person with the flu shows certain familiar physical symptoms, such as a fever and runny nose, someone suffering from gender dysphoria demonstrates some recognizable emotional symptoms.

Usually the first of these symptoms to manifest itself is the feeling of being born in the wrong body. As one noted physician puts it, there is "a marked incongruence between the patient's experienced or expressed gender and his or her assigned gender." This disparity between biological gender and inward emotional feelings results in a "strong desire to be of the other gender."[16] Or else the person insists that he or she already is of that other gender.

This feeling that one's assigned body parts do not reflect one's actual gender can result in the frustration, worry, and distress associated with gender dysphoria. In some people these feelings of discomfort can be very strong, even severe. It is not unusual, for instance, for the person to often feel anxious and depressed.

Dangerously Miserable and Fearful

Indeed, clinical depression is one of the most common symptoms of gender dysphoria. This form of depression, the world-famous Mayo Clinic explains, "isn't the same as depression caused by a loss, such as the death of a loved one." It is normal to feel extremely sad over such a loss, but such feelings are typically temporary. In contrast, someone with clinical depression, a spokesperson for the clinic says, is stricken on a regular, ongoing basis with a combination of debilitating effects. In children and teens, one of these is constant irritability. Two others are "reduced interest or feeling no pleasure in all or most activities" and "significant weight loss when not dieting."[17] Also associated with this severe form of depression are difficulty sleeping, fatigue and loss of energy, feelings of worthlessness or guilt, trouble concentrating or making decisions, and recurring thoughts of committing suicide.

At the age of fifteen, Jay Maddock experienced most of these gloomy feelings, at first without understanding why. The idea that he might be transgender did not occur to him because he was unfamiliar with both that term and concept. One thing Maddock did know was that he often had a strange feeling that he was living in the wrong body. He had been born with female genitals, yet in his mind he felt more male than female. "I wasn't comfortable in my body," he says. "I wore baggier and baggier clothes to hide my body. I didn't see anyone like me. The closest I could see were Ellen DeGeneres and Rosie O'Donnell, who were more masculine and gay. So I thought that must be me."[18]

In time, however, the confused, unhappy young man realized that he was not gay. After he described his feelings to some friends, they told him he did not sound like a gay person. Someone suggested he might be transgender, which spurred him to go online and read numerous articles about the condition. Clearly,

15

One teen, who was trying to come to terms with feelings of living in the wrong body, searched for role models. He thought of openly gay comedian Ellen DeGeneres (pictured) but her situation did not seem to correspond with his.

he concluded with a sudden rush of realization, he was indeed a transgender person.

But what could he do about that, Maddock wondered? He knew he had to do something because he felt he was becoming dangerously miserable and fearful. "I was becoming more and more depressed," he recalls.

So I was either going to come out as transgender or not be able to exist in the world anymore. It was the New Year and I realized I didn't want to waste another year. I had this huge panic attack, realizing what I was feeling was not going away and I was going to deal with it one way or another. I'd either take a deep breath and come out and take the risk of losing people, or I would risk losing *myself*.[19]

Mental Transitioning and Cross-Dressing

Fortunately for him, Maddock did not lose himself. Instead, he came out to his family and closest friends and told them he was transgender. Not only that, but he also told them that he suffered from a condition that doctors called gender dysphoria, characterized by constant and severe emotional distress and pain.

All of those with whom Maddock shared his painful secret were sympathetic to his plight. That allowed him to make a crucial mental transition that was essential to his emotional well-being. He had learned that another common symptom of gender dysphoria is a strong desire to identify with, to become, and/or to be treated like a member of the other gender. He harbored that very desire—in his case to be able to say he was a boy and to be treated as one. This act of mental transition "started the process of falling in love with myself," he remembers.

> "I was either going to come out as transgender or not be able to exist in the world anymore."[19]
>
> —Fifteen-year-old Jay Maddock

If you can imagine the start of a relationship with someone you're head over heels in love with—that giddiness every time you get to see them. There's something similar about transitioning and starting to see yourself externally the way you've always known yourself internally, of finally getting to meet the person you've always had inside.[20]

Maddock began to dress as a male. He had not cross-dressed when he was a teenager still wrestling with why he was so unhappy. But in his extensive reading about the transgender phenomenon, he had learned that cross-dressing (when a male dresses, briefly or at length, as a female or vice versa) is a common symptom of gender dysphoria. (Some transgender people cross-dress even when they do *not* suffer from gender dysphoria.) Many adolescents who struggle with being transgender secretly, or in some cases openly, wear the clothes of the gender opposite their own assigned gender.

Heather Young, now an adult who identifies as a woman, was one of those young cross-dressers. Her mother, Coleen, and father, David, had early on recognized that something of a serious nature was bothering their son. "When [he] was seven or eight years old, we caught [him] cross-dressing," Coleen recollects. He had

> done the typical dress-up things, but it didn't seem like anything unusual. But the fact that [he] started doing it in secret told us something else was going on. My husband and I thought maybe [he] was gay and tried to take [him] to a gender therapist. [He] wasn't ready, so we gave [him] some space. But we weren't comfortable seeing [him] in feminine apparel. We told [him] it would be okay to dress that way, but only in [his] bedroom. I wish now we would have handled that differently. But you can't go back.[21]

A Cloudy Area of Confusion and Fear

Another very common symptom of both transgenderism and gender dysphoria in young people is a person's strong preference or desire to play with the toys designed for children of the gender opposite the one that person was assigned at birth. That is, biological boys who are transgender usually enjoy playing with stereotypical girls' toys. Similarly, biological girls who are transgender most often like playing with stereotypical boys' toys.

Some children enjoy playing with toys designed for the opposite gender. This preference can be a symptom of transgenderism and gender dysphoria—but that is not always the case.

Research has shown that the healthiest approach for a transgender child is for him or her to be allowed to play with whatever toys he or she desires. Far too often, however, parents or other supervising adults—frequently well-meaning ones—assume the opposite is true. They think it is likely unhealthy for girls to play with boys' toys and vice versa. So they disallow children from playing with the toys associated with the opposite gender.

Christabel Edwards, a media consultant, remembers being in that position as a child. "I am a transgender woman," she says. "I was classified as male at birth and I transitioned to female in my thirties." Edwards recalls being in a playgroup at age two at the local village hall: "I was playing with toys along with some other children in a side room off the main hall when one of the staff

Educating the Community

After her son identified as a female, who later came to call herself Heather, Coleen Young worked with various community agencies and groups in her town to educate their members about transgenderism and gender dysphoria. She was able to obtain the understanding and support of most parents, school officials, teachers, church leaders, and others. Young explains her approach, saying,

If you haven't been around trans people it can be hard to understand. So I'd urge anyone who doesn't understand to talk to transgender people. Let them tell their story. Even if you don't understand or agree, they still deserve the respect any other individual deserves. I'd also encourage schools to learn how they should treat transgender people. There weren't any transgender students at my school when I was teaching, and just a few years later almost every high school has students coming out as transgender. As long as they have some support at the high school, that seems to help so much. Trans people are successful [in life] if they have supportive parents [and other community members]. The 40 percent rate of trans people who have attempted suicide breaks my heart. It's so important for parents to support their kids. It does so much to make their kids happy and successful.

Quoted in Amy Lynn Smith, "Coleen's Story: Unconditional Love and Support," *Eclectablog* (blog), April 6, 2016. www.eclectablog.com.

came in. She picked me up and took me from the [girls'] toys I was playing with and put me down next to [some boys'] toys on the other side of the room, so I went back to where I'd been enjoying myself."[22]

Soon the same adult who had moved the little boy returned, found he was again playing with girls' toys, and moved him once more. This was repeated several times until finally the adult slapped the child and scolded him, saying it was bad for him to play with girls' toys. "Being punished before I was three for wanting to play in the 'wrong' role," Edwards states, "left me in a horrible limbo," a cloudy, scary area of emotional confusion and fear. She continues,

I had learned in my formative years that any expression of my femininity was "naughty," which prevented me from alerting my own liberal-minded parents, who I now know would have been accepting and supportive. It set me up for a lifetime of loneliness, lack of social bonding and being an outcast. . . . I'm still shocked that as a child I was prevented from expressing myself in a safe and supervised environment where I was doing no harm either to myself or others.[23]

Reaching a Proper Diagnosis

Doctors and other experts have observed a number of other symptoms of gender dysphoria (or in some cases just being transgender) in children and teens. One is choosing to play only with friends of the gender with which the transgender child identifies. Another example is refusing to urinate in the physical position—either standing or sitting—that children of one's assigned gender typically do. A young person with severe gender dysphoria may even talk about ridding him- or herself of the genitals with which he or she was born. It is also common for teenagers with gender dysphoria to avoid all sexual situations. This is because they are not yet sure who they are, sexually speaking, and do not want to have sex until they do.

"[Being forced to hide who I really was] set me up for a lifetime of loneliness, lack of social bonding and being an outcast."[23]

—Media consultant Christabel Edwards

Recognizing the symptoms of gender dysphoria is important because it allows doctors, parents, and the sufferers themselves to reach a proper diagnosis. A diagnosis is a conclusion or verdict that states that someone does definitely suffer from some sort of ailment. Knowing that a young person has gender dysphoria is crucial, partly because that person can now address the causes of the disorder. He or she can also seek treatment. Otherwise, the person may well face many years of discontent or out-and-out misery.

Indeed, experts point out that individuals with gender dysphoria have a higher rate of mental health conditions in general than the general population. One study found that at least 71 percent of people with gender dysphoria will be diagnosed with some other mental health problem in their lifetimes. In addition to clinical depression, these problems include mood and anxiety disorders, substance abuse, eating disorders, and suicide attempts. The main goals, therefore, doctors say, should be to diagnose gender dysphoria as early as possible, discover the causes of this distress, and find the best treatment for it.

CHAPTER TWO

What Causes Gender Dysphoria?

In the briefest possible terms, a person suffers from gender dysphoria because of serious difficulty in coping with the fact that he or she is transgender. So in a very real sense, gender dysphoria is caused by being transgender in the first place. Thus, the causes of transgenderism and gender dysphoria are more or less the same.

Medical professionals point out that the exact causes of transgenderism remain unclear. Nevertheless, doctors and other experts have come a long way in recent years toward understanding what is behind this phenomenon. Despite this, a handful of experts still cling to prior assumptions about transgenderism's causes, which the vast majority of scientists now reject. So it is important to look at those outdated assumptions along with the newer, more accepted theory.

Initially, for example, doctors thought that simply being transgender was a type of mental illness. A transgender person was said to be suffering from "gender identity disorder." This allowed medical authorities to "describe the entire trans community as disordered, delusional, and mentally ill," says Zack Ford, of the Center for American Progress. "In some cases," he goes on, that diagnosis was "used to discriminate against trans people, with claims that they are unfit parents or employees."[24]

However, continuing research showed that this way of looking at transgenderism was incorrect. In 2012 the American Psychiatric Association board of trustees made historic changes to the organization's well-known manual, the *Diagnostic and Statistical Manual of Mental Disorders*. Often called the *DSM-5* for short, the manual no longer classifies transgender people as mentally ill. Instead, the medical community now regards that condition as a normal deviation in the human mental spectrum.

The manual's new language did acknowledge that some transgender people can and do suffer from a debilitating condition. Namely, they might feel significant distress and discomfort from trying to deal with being transgender. If so, the manual now states, they have a condition called gender dysphoria.

The "Genitals and Upbringing" Theory

Just as medical authorities were originally wrong in classifying transgender people as mentally ill, those authorities seem to have been initially mistaken about what causes transgenderism. For decades the assumption was that there was a fairly simple explanation. Like many other experts, noted scientist and authority on transgenderism Lynn Conway calls it the "genitals and upbringing" theory. About the "genitals" part, she says, "conventional wisdom says that people are either boys who grow up to become men, or they are girls who grow up to become women." In this shortsighted view, she points out, "there are only two possibilities, and you are either one or the other. It's obvious at birth from your 'genital sex' and that's all there is to it!"[25]

> "Conventional wisdom says that people are either boys who grow up to become men, or they are girls who grow up to become women."[25]
>
> —Scientist and transgender activist Lynn Conway

The "upbringing" part of this outdated theory, Conway continues, in a sense was closely related to the genitals part. First, it was seen as normal and expected that a child born with a penis would be raised as a boy. Moreover, the theory "predicted that a child having a penis and raised as a boy would grow up to have a normal male gender identity, independent of his genes." (A person's genes are the microscopic units in cells that carry the traits one inherits from one's parents.) Similarly, the theory stated, "a child having a vagina and raised as a girl will grow up to have a female gender identity, independent of her genes."[26]

Why some kids come to see themselves as transgender and others do not is not entirely clear. Experts do know that those who feel they are being raised in the wrong gender often experience extreme mental anguish, which can lead to gender dysphoria.

Thus, the key to a boy's or girl's natural and comfortable gender identity was thought to be that child's upbringing. All a set of parents had to do was to raise their son as a boy and/or their daughter as a girl. As long as this was done in a straightforward manner, everything about the child's feelings relating to gender would automatically work out for the better.

That is, all would work out in a positive way as long as nothing abnormal was involved. Experts did recognize that in a very small number of cases something was amiss with a child's gender identity. Either a boy felt that he identified more as a girl, or a female felt more normal and comfortable identifying as a male, Conway explains. In such cases, she says, the experts "assumed that something 'went wrong' in the child's upbringing, or that the child was mentally disturbed or delusional in some way (i.e., 'mentally ill')."[27]

The Church Turned Its Back

Jayne Locke now identifies herself as a woman. But she grew up as a boy in an era when the general assumption was that being transgender was a matter of personal choice or faulty upbringing. People generally lacked an understanding of the topic, and partly for that reason tended either to condemn transgender individuals or to shy away from them. In Locke's case those who turned their backs on her included fellow churchgoers, whom she cared greatly about. Locke remembers that things came to a head when a visiting female evangelist came to preach and singled her out from the congregation's all-female praise and worship group.

> As the sermon ended, it was customary for the praise and worship team to go back on the platform to play music. As I went to take my place, the evangelist looked me in the eye and on the microphone said, "Sir, I do not remember inviting you up here." I was mortified, but I said it was time to play music and she repeated herself. I left the platform in tears. The following week, I came back to church and everyone apologized to me. But a few weeks later a man who was an elder in the church showed up and had a fit. I became such a controversy in the church that I was asked to leave.

Quoted in Amy Lynn Smith, "Jayne's Story: Revealing the Woman Within," *Eclectablog* (blog), May 17, 2016. www.eclectablog.com.

"I Was Defective"

One transgender person who grew up when her condition was seen as a mental illness was Jayne Locke, now in her sixties. Locke was born with normal-looking male genitals, so her parents naturally raised the child as a boy. However, she recalls,

> I knew I was different. I didn't have the same proclivities [likes and dislikes] as other boys and I didn't like doing the things they did. My preferences were much more to be with the girls. But when you're a child, if you look like a boy and you're called a boy, the girls think you have cooties. They want nothing to do with you. [As a result] a lot of my time was spent alone.[28]

Moreover, growing up during the 1950s, Locke had to contend with the labels and name-calling then widely associated with little boys who did not act the way society expected them to act. Although raised as a boy, at times "he" acted "a bit feminine." She reminds people that in those days almost no one knew anything about transgenderism. So people frequently assumed that boys who had feminine traits were gay. It was often seen as "fun and games for people to go out and beat up homosexuals," Locke recollects.[29]

Locke did not want to be persecuted for being gay, she recalls. So as a little boy she did whatever was necessary to hide her real feelings from other people and act as "male" as possible. It was constantly emotionally difficult because society seemed to have decided that people like her were bad. In fact, she came to accept that labeling herself. "I kept falling for the same thing that had been drilled into me," the grown-up Locke says. There seemed to be no doubt that "something was wrong with me, that I was defective, that I was a pervert—the whole thing." For these reasons, Locke kept her gender identity issues to herself: "I didn't even want to admit it to myself. That was the single biggest problem: coming to grips with it myself and how to deal with it."[30]

> "I kept falling for the same thing that had been drilled into me. [It was that] something was wrong with me, that I was defective, that I was a pervert."[30]
>
> —Transgender woman Jayne Locke

Flaws in the Standard Theory?

During the era in which Locke grew up, the vast majority of experts on human sexuality thought that the way to correct such a "defect" in a child's gender-related feelings was to take her or him to a psychiatrist. The assumption was that this would help because psychiatrists are therapists who specialize in, among other things, mental disorders, and the theory of "genitals and upbringing" held that transgenderism was a mental disturbance or disorder. As such, doctors assumed, in all likelihood it could be reversed or cured by a doctor versed in such things.

As time went on, however, it became increasingly clear that the genitals and upbringing theory had been little more than a supposition. Very little serious research had been done on transgenderism before that theory became standard among medical authorities. Moreover, some scientists began to question various aspects of the theory because they did not seem to make sense.

For example, the theory's central tenet—that gender is determined by upbringing—seemed to be refuted by a number of real-life cases that came to light. For that major principle to be true, bringing an anatomical boy up as a male should always result in a healthy, mentally stable person who easily accepts himself as a boy. Yet doctors saw more than a few families in which boys firmly raised as boys eventually became convinced that they were girls on the inside.

Furthermore, the genitals and upbringing theory did not account for transgender people growing up in highly homophobic families. That is, when the parents and other relatives constantly emphasize that it is wrong for a boy to feel or act in feminine ways, they place extra stress on the importance of masculine thought and behavior. In such cases—assuming the theory is true—a boy brought up in a homophobic home should never become transgender. Yet experts found a number of transgender people who had been raised in such homes.

One man, who does not want to reveal his name, came from that very kind of home. "The social environment I grew up in was extremely homophobic," he explains. "As is the format for many effeminate males, my tribulations [misfortunes or suffering] escalated at high school." There, he goes on, "I was exposed to taunts and bullying." Since that time, he states, "my relationship with men in my family has deteriorated so drastically that the defamation [insults] I received at school was proportionate to that which I received at home."[31]

> "My relationship with men in my family has deteriorated so drastically that the defamation [insults] I received at school was proportionate to that which I received at home."[31]
>
> —An anonymous transgender man

The young man who wrote these words left home while still a teenager. In the fifteen years that followed, he says, he transitioned into a female and spent most of his time "finding who I am." The little contact he had with family members was mostly discouraging. "They still refer to me as 'He' and call me by a name that is totally alien to me, my christened name," he writes. "I believe the lack of family support and understanding" has increased

> the difficulties of being and becoming transgender. It is not surprising so many of us lack self-esteem, are depressed, and resort to drug escapism. But many of us come through the tunnel to the light on the other side, stronger and able to guide [others like us] on their journey.[32]

Enter the Brain and Bodily Hormones

As medical experts studied more and more cases like this one, the vast majority increasingly rejected the genitals and upbringing theory. Moreover, from the 1980s on, more extensive and detailed research was conducted on the human brain and the many chemicals that it and other human body parts regularly manufacture. Study after study suggested that people become transgender as a result of biological causes, especially those involving the body's production of hormones. In the words of Dr. Ananya Mandal, a leader in the field, gender identity—and gender dysphoria along with it—appears to derive from a person's development before birth. According to the bulk of existing research, she states, the "development that determines biological sex happens in the mother's womb."[33]

Mandal and most other scientists have come to believe that one major way transgenderism comes about is when the brain hormones that decide someone's gender fail to function effectively in the womb. As a result of this failure, that person may come to have serious questions about what his or her gender really is. Stated in the most basic, simple way, that individual's anatomical, or genital, gender may not match up with his or her brain-centered, or neurological, gender. Hence, these experts came to see, a child

29

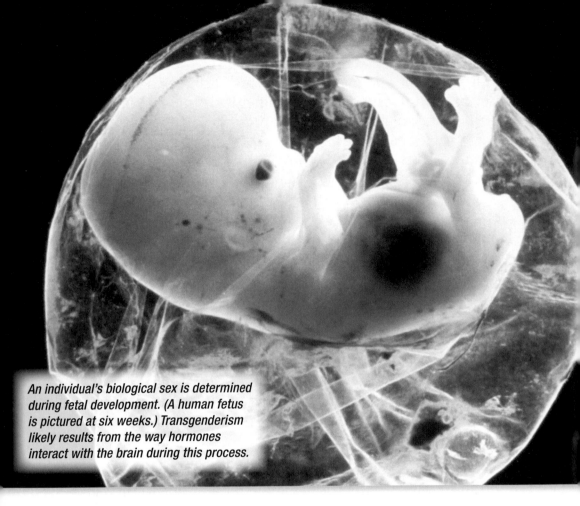

An individual's biological sex is determined during fetal development. (A human fetus is pictured at six weeks.) Transgenderism likely results from the way hormones interact with the brain during this process.

born with a boy's genitals, or anatomical sex, may have the neurological gender of a girl, or vice versa.

The actual facts about the underlying causes of transgenderism and gender dysphoria are far from simple, however. In addition, not only are these conditions highly complex, but new discoveries about them are also made regularly. Indeed, "this area is under rapid development," Lynn Conway points out.[34]

Conway is often called upon to sort through this mass of complicated knowledge and explain the gender-related conditions to nonscientists in an easy-to-understand manner. Maybe once in every two hundred to four hundred births, she begins, "something must go amiss in the early stages of pregnancy,"[35] when a person is still a fetus in his or her mother's womb. Normally, the body releases certain hormones that help to determine whether the person will become a boy or a girl.

In the case of a transgender individual, however, those hormones do not affect the fetus's brain in the ways they do in a majority of pregnancies. In this small minority of cases, Conway continues, "children are born having a brain-sex (neurological sex) and innate gender identity opposite to that indicated both by their genes and their genitalia. Since these infants look normal, they will be raised in the wrong gender for their brain-sex."[36]

Crucial Male Hormonal Surges

To understand the cause of transgenderism, therefore, scientists must search at the chemical and molecular level and look at the hormones at work in the fetus's brain and other developing body parts. Among the more important of these hormones, studies have revealed, are those that help determine if a developing fetus will become an anatomical boy or an anatomical girl.

All fetuses technically start out as females. Only after exposure to surges of certain hormones, principally androgens like testosterone, does the fetus transform, anatomically speaking, into a male. If those surges do not occur, the developing child goes on to become an anatomical female.

This initial hormonal surge, or lack thereof, takes place between the sixth and twelfth weeks of pregnancy. By the twelfth week, therefore, the child's tendency to become anatomically either a boy or a girl has been determined. However, the brain's hormonal development toward gender identity has not yet occurred. In fact, a new surge of hormones transforms the brain in the second half of a typical pregnancy. These substances include more androgens.

If this new surge of hormones happens with the proper proportions of those substances, the fetus's brain-centered gender identity will strengthen the already existing anatomical gender. In other words, a fetus with female genitals will develop a normal, or average, female brain chemistry. Similarly, a fetus with male genitals will develop a normal, or average, male brain chemistry.

The potential problem lies in the timing of these two major hormonal surges. As one researcher puts it, "the fact that the brain and the genitals develop at different times in the womb means that a misalignment between the genitals and brain may develop."[37] One way this can happen is if higher-than-normal levels of male hormones flood the brain of a fetus that already features female genital anatomy. In that case the brain may take on male characteristics. That person will go on to be born an anatomical female who may later exhibit male social tendencies and male personality features. She may then feel like a boy trapped in a female body.

The Role of Maternal Hormones

A different scenario can occur sometimes as well. In this case during the second half of the pregnancy, lower-than-normal levels of male hormones enter the brain of a fetus that already features male genital anatomy. If this takes place, the fetus's "masculinization," or transformation into a normal male with male brain chemistry, will be disrupted. The fetus will go on to be born a baby with a penis and testicles. But as he grows up he may not identify himself as a male. According to Dr. L. Fleming Fallon of Bowling Green State University, those

> male hormonal surges must occur not only in sufficient amounts, but also during a short window of time to cause masculinization of the developing infant. If there is insufficient androgen, the hormone primarily responsible for masculinization, or the surge comes too early or too late, the developing infant may be incompletely masculinized.[38]

Logically, the next question to address is how or why such disruptions occur in the average, expected flow of androgen and other crucial hormones within the fetal brain. Scientists say that this interference in the normal process can come from a variety of sources. One is a disorder in the mother's endocrine system, the collection of bodily glands that produce her hormones. If one or more of her glands happens to be producing too little or too much of a certain hormone, one result can be a disruption in the normal flow of hormones within her womb.

Another common source of shortages of key hormones within the fetal brain is stress affecting the mother. Medically speaking,

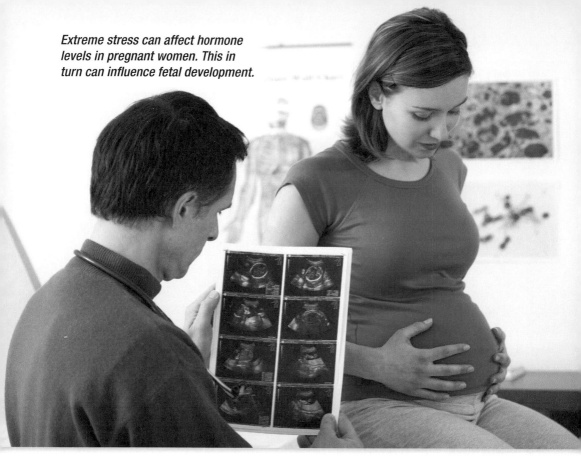

Extreme stress can affect hormone levels in pregnant women. This in turn can influence fetal development.

stress is a combination of physical, mental, and emotional strains or tensions a person may feel when things in his or her life are not going well. This condition can affect levels of maternal hormones, too. When a pregnant mother is stressed out, it can cause one or more of her hormone-producing glands to over- or under-produce. In turn, this can have direct effects on her developing fetus, including some related to gender identity.

Other sources of disruptions in normal fetal hormone flow include certain medications or illegal drugs the mother might take, or toxic substances she may consume without knowing it.

The Onset of Dysphoria

In whatever manner a person becomes transgender, he or she may or may not end up experiencing gender dysphoria—distress over not fitting into "normal" society. Many individuals who do suffer from that condition encounter numerous negative consequences in nearly all aspects of their lives. "Being raised in the

Mistaking Transgender for Gay

One of the more common misconceptions about the cause of transgenderism is that it is a form of homosexuality, or being gay. Noted scientist and transgender activist Lynn Conway explains here why that is not true. (She sometimes uses the term *transsexual*, which she says is more or less synonymous with *transgender*.)

Transgenderism [is] most often confused with simply being gay, and in fact confused with being "really, really gay." The first thing that pops into the people's heads when they hear that someone is transsexual is, "Wow, I didn't know 'he' was gay." It's easy to see how people might jump to this conclusion. Seeing a male-to-female transgender woman with a straight man as her partner, they simply think that she is (or was) a "gay man." They jump to the conclusion that "he" changed sex simply in order to attract men as partners. However, this is a totally mistaken idea rooted in ignorance about gender identity. . . . Now, here's the deal: A gay man has a male gender identity. He is attracted to males who also have a male gender identity, and who are attracted to him because he is a male. The last thing on earth that a gay man would want to do is change sex and become a woman. To do so would be a catastrophically self-destructive act, because of his male gender identity and his love of masculinity both in himself and in his partners.

Lynn Conway, "Basic TG/TS/IS Information." http://ai.eecs.umich.edu/people/conway/TS/TS.html.

wrong gender," Conway remarks, often causes these individuals severe "mental anguish as they grow up."[39]

The degree to which a person feels and experiences such dysphoria varies widely from individual to individual. Some do not experience it at all, while others are so upset by it that they are driven to suicide. Studies show that to a great degree it depends on how the person is perceived and treated by family, friends, and society in general. As Conway explains, sometimes young transgender women have an easier time adjusting to the "normal" world around them than their male counterparts do. "The girl who feels like a boy," she says, can often become a "tomboy" and not get criticized for that. In fact she may even gain approval for being outgoing and aggressive and tomboyish in our male-dominated society. However, she may still feel the same degree of gender angst about her assigned gender role as does the male-to-female transgender boy.[40]

As for those "feminine little boys who really should have been girls," Conway continues, "fathers especially will make every effort to 'straighten out' such boys. The feminine boy is mistakenly thought of as 'pre-homosexual.' Every effort is then made to 'save the boy from that fate.'"[41] Not surprisingly, boys who must endure these sorts of pressures will develop worse cases of gender dysphoria than they would have otherwise.

An example of how upsetting gender dysphoria can be for such a person is the case of Char Davenport. She was born an anatomical boy, but for a long time felt trapped in the wrong body. Davenport recalls a conversation she had with her father on their house's front porch, in which he insisted that his son play baseball. Davenport did not want to play and as the father continued to insist, she remembers eventually being distraught and in tears.

> I was so panicked and I said, "I am a girl!" We went back and forth, and I told him I wanted to be like this girl I knew. And he said, "You don't want to be a girl. Girls are stupid." I remember looking at him and thinking I'd lost this argument. I knew I'd lost myself at that moment, that I was gone. That was the end of me. I didn't think of it in those terms yet, but I knew it was a huge loss. I remember thinking, "Who am I? Why is this happening? What's wrong with my dad—why can't he see me?"[42]

This feeling of being lost and unable to relate to one's own parent is only one of countless negative experiences reported by transgender people doing their best to survive in a world that has just begun to understand their plight.

CHAPTER THREE

What Is It Like to Live with Gender Dysphoria?

Lynn Conway and other experts on transgender people and issues believe that most trans individuals do experience gender dysphoria to one degree or another at some point in life. This puts them at a clear disadvantage when compared to the majority of people, who feel no disconnect between their anatomical gender and the gender their minds tell them they are. For transgender people, Conway explains,

> living without having a properly assigned gender produces a nightmarish separation from the dance of life. Whether it's dating, finding love, courting, marrying, raising children, and generally doing all the little everyday things that continually celebrate one's own gender, the transgendered are often left stranded on the sidelines, to watch as spectators. Or worse yet, while feeling ugly and ludicrous in their male social appearance, they are forced to "act out," empty of all feeling, a role that is alien to their inner female nature.[43]

One transgender female, Sophia Gubb, provides an analogy for this odd feeling of having two different roles in society—one based on outer appearance, the other based on inner feelings. She notes that when making the movie *Cloud Atlas,* actor Susan Sarandon played both a woman and a man. Wearing the heavy makeup that had transformed her into her male role, she found it strange when looking in the mirror. "Who is this person?" Sarandon asked. "That was just a startling experience, you know, to not recognize yourself at all."

Gubb contends that in a sense "Susan Sarandon was describing gender dysphoria!" While the actress "seemed to find it an interesting experience," Gubb continues,

> I doubt she would enjoy it if she was forced to experience this every day. Gender dysphoria is weird and wouldn't make a bad experience if it were just once. But add repetition, inescapability, and the connected frustration of not being able to be yourself and you have a recipe for hell. I expect, also, that feeling disconnected from your own sense of self must not be too bad for a short while, but long-term it seriously and genuinely takes away from your ability to function in life.[44]

"Not Sorry for Being Me"

A major part of a trans person's living on the "sidelines" of life, as Conway puts it, is having to constantly deal with people's reactions to learning he or she is transgender. So often there is a lack of understanding by many of those "cis" persons. (*Cisgender* is a term describing people whose anatomical gender matches their gender identity.) Frequently, even well-meaning cisgender people who do not intend to add to someone's feelings of gender dysphoria are so ignorant of the issue that they say the wrong thing. Another trans person, who writes a blog titled *Tarnished Sophia* (and chooses not to reveal her last name), gives typical examples of what she and some of her transgender friends have experienced:

> This is what it's like every single day for someone like myself. Reactions are quite varied too. "Just get over it." "You know, you should accept who you really, truly are." "Nobody actually feels that way." "You're such a freak." "Why do you hate your own sex?" "Why are you being so difficult?" And my personal favorite: "You should have sex more, so your partner can 'remind' you that you're female."[45]

Transgender Youth and Adults Experience Many Difficulties

In a survey of more than six thousand transgender people in the United States, large numbers reported experiencing harassment, rejection, and other difficulties that complicate daily life. Among transgender youth, physical assault represented the second most common problem behind harassment. And, among transgender adults, suicide attempts are far more common than in the general population.

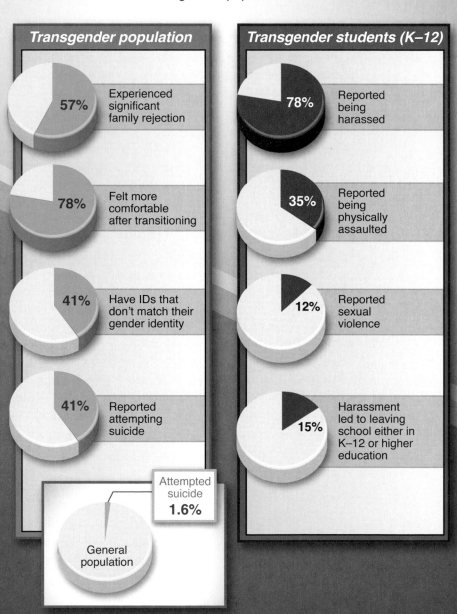

Transgender population

- 57% — Experienced significant family rejection
- 78% — Felt more comfortable after transitioning
- 41% — Have IDs that don't match their gender identity
- 41% — Reported attempting suicide

Transgender students (K–12)

- 78% — Reported being harassed
- 35% — Reported being physically assaulted
- 12% — Reported sexual violence
- 15% — Harassment led to leaving school either in K–12 or higher education

Attempted suicide **1.6%** — General population

Source: Eli Francovich, "A Transgender Child's Journey," *Spokesman-Review*, June 3, 2016. www.spokesman.com.

The problem, the writer goes on, is that while the majority of these cisgender people believe they are helping the situation, they actually are not. Being transgender and suffering from gender dysphoria are not connected to simple switches that can be turned on and off, she points out. "It's not a choice to feel more in tune with the opposite sex," she says. Nor did she voluntarily choose "to have severe difficulties relating to and having friendships." Rather,

> "I have always felt repulsed and horrified by the idea of getting pregnant."[46]
>
> —A transgender individual who created the blog *Tarnished Sophia*

I have always felt like a male, and have never grown out of it. I have always felt repulsed and horrified by the idea of getting pregnant. [Moreover] I will always be this way, and will live my life as best I can. I am sorry if that makes others uncomfortable, but I'm not sorry for being me.[46]

From Keeping Secrets to Coming Out

Marika K. Jackson is a transgender person who was born an anatomical boy but later transitioned into a woman. Like the transgender blogger, Jackson knows firsthand what it is like to have childhood difficulties maintaining friendships. She also had trouble meeting society's expectations of how young boys should act.

As far back in her childhood as she can remember, Jackson says, she felt unhappy without understanding why she felt that way. In a simplistic attempt to explain it, she figured she was somehow defective as a boy. "My unhappiness," she remarks, might best be

described as being "maleness dysphoria". From quite an early age, seven or eight years old, until well into my teens, I was acutely and painfully aware that my temperament and my interests were at odds with those of other boys around my age, including my younger brother and his many friends.[47]

Jackson's family lived in a semirural region of England "with many opportunities for adventurous boys to amuse themselves," she recalls. "And I would sometimes join my brother and his friends to do just that. I much preferred, however, to hang out with the few girls of the neighborhood." Those girls played games young Jackson found much more interesting than the ones his brother and other male companions played. Moreover, while the boys enjoyed certain action-filled comic books, Jackson preferred ones specifically designed for little girls. But when he asked his mother to help him find more such female-oriented comics, he was in for a rude awakening. "She made it quite clear," he remembers,

> that that would not happen and then went on to suggest that I should spend less time with my girlfriends and try to join in with the boys more. It was probably as a result of that moment that the discomfort with my identity germinated in my psyche, the notion that it would be wonderful to be a girl. I became very emotional throughout my early-teens and I would cry at the drop of a hat, much to the exasperation of my parents, especially my father who, in every macho way, was a "man's man."[48]

To ensure his masculinity, Jackson's parents sent him to an all-boys school. But he did poorly there. So when he was fifteen his father persuaded him to join England's air force, the RAF, as an engineering apprentice. The young man served in that branch of the service for fourteen years. He got along well with young women in the service, so his parents and brother assumed he had straightened out and was now a "normal" male. They did not realize that he felt comfortable socializing with women but did not want to actually date them.

Eventually, however, Jackson met a woman named Kate and de-

"I became very emotional throughout my early-teens and I would cry at the drop of a hat, much to the exasperation of my parents."[48]

—English transgender woman Marika K. Jackson

A Heartfelt Coming-Out Letter

Born a male, Marika K. Jackson grew up as a boy and as an adult got married, raised children, and served in the military. All through those years, she felt in her mind that she was actually a woman. So later in life she transitioned to a female persona, Marika. She says she found it extremely hard to tell her siblings the truth and has published the heartfelt letter in which she came out to her brother, David. Here are a few short excerpts from the letter:

Dear David,

This is one of the most difficult letters I have ever had to write. I had to do it this way, however, so that, after you have carefully considered what I have to tell you, you'll have enough information on which to base a decision as to whether you could still be comfortable with me as your brother. . . . My problem turns out to be a medical condition known as Gender Dysphoria, possibly as a result of incomplete fetal development prior to birth. Although my physical sex is male, my gender (brain sex) is female. Put simply, a female psyche trapped in a male body. . . . This letter is not a pathetic plea for sympathy or support. Personally, I don't need either. In fact, I've never felt better about myself. I'm experiencing something that few others have, or ever will; the rare opportunity to be physically re-born. . . . I have no feelings of embarrassment, shame or guilt. I just want to be open and honest with everyone.

Marika K. Jackson, "My Struggle with Identity," Gender Centre, October 2013. www.gendercentre.org.au.

cided to marry her. She had two young children from a prior marriage, so he was now suddenly a father, even though deep down inside he still felt more like a woman than a man. Years elapsed and Jackson often suffered from deep depression before he finally mustered the nerve to tell his wife the truth about his feelings. He told Kate, as well as his brother and other family members, that he wanted to spend the rest of his life as a woman. Fortunately for him, just about everyone he came out to turned out to be understanding and supportive. "Kate has now accepted my course as inevitable," Jackson explains, and "she has been enormously relieved to find that friends have not fallen away."[49]

Secrecy, Tension, and Release

The vast majority of transgender people in England, the United States, Canada, and other Western countries have gone or are now going through a process similar to Jackson's. At first they keep their true gender identity secret from everyone they know. Then after the passage of some time, they finally come out to their loved ones. That time period varies in length from person to person. Jackson waited well into her adult years to come out, but some trans people do so when they are in their teens or even younger.

For many of these tortured individuals, the guilt and sadness over keeping their major secret, for however long, brings on bouts of gender dysphoria. Indeed, the inability to express themselves in an honest, open, and healthy way weighs hard on them. Lapsing into episodes of anxiety and depression is common, as is coming to harshly judge or even to hate themselves. One trans person who prefers to remain anonymous says,

> My identity remained hidden behind closed doors, behind walls, in prison. Not even I would allow myself to embrace the sanctity of self. I lived to define myself in the eyes of all around me. A prisoner by virtue of my selfishness. Craving acceptance from others yet unable to find the balance of selfishness and selflessness required through acceptance of myself.[50]

Trans people have tried to cope in many ways with the stress triggered by their months or years of secrecy and dysphoria. One of the more common outlets they find for relieving that stress is cross-dressing—when a male dresses, briefly or at length, as a female or vice versa. Janet Fletcher, a male-to-female transgender person, recalls how her original episodes of cross-dressing came about. An extremely mixed-up, confused, and miserable young man, he kept his inner female feelings a secret. The stress drove him to attempt suicide, which failed. Then he met a young woman and married her when he was in his early twenties.

The serious stress stemming from the young man's gender dysphoria continued to build. Finally, he found that cross-dressing helped to release the "tensions I felt back then."[51] In fact, medical experts say, for trans people cross-dressing can relieve stress because it allows them to explore and enjoy their hidden gender feelings, whether they be female or male in nature. Marika Jackson, for example, acknowledges dressing in women's clothes in secret when he was still male and his wife, Kate, was away at work. "I would take photographs of myself" in those clothes, Jackson recalls. "I even went out" and cross-dressed in public "on a couple of evenings. I really was quite convincing."[52]

> "My identity remained hidden behind closed doors, behind walls, in prison. Not even I would allow myself to embrace the sanctity of self."[50]
>
> —An anonymous transgender individual

Janet Fletcher found herself in the same position when still a young man. "About eighteen months into our relationship," she says, "I introduced cross-dressing behavior into our marriage." And Fletcher's wife, "poor conservative rural nurse she was, was introduced to the real world. Her reaction? She hated it. She hated it with a passion. But she allowed me to do a very limited amount of cross-dressing."[53]

Transgender People and School Sports

In addition to coming out to family and friends or simply dealing day-to-day with loved ones, transgender people face the often difficult necessity of interacting with strangers. Many trans individuals point out that society has erected certain barriers against them. Often these take the form of rules that make it hard for them to take part in various public activities.

One of these activities is school athletics. "Currently," the Women's Sports Foundation reports,

> only a few school sports governing organizations have adopted policies addressing the inclusion of transgender athletes, although many more are beginning to explore the issue and to recognize the need for such policies. Failure to develop informed and fair policies leaves school athletic programs unprepared to respond to the increased probability that a transgender student will seek to join a school team.[54]

The foundation emphasizes that schools are obligated to allow trans teens to participate in sports under the Equal Protection Clause of the US Constitution. Furthermore,

> ideally, transgender athletes should have access to the facilities that are available to other athletes of the gender with which they identify. Athletes who desire increased privacy should be provided with accommodations that best meet their needs and privacy concerns, such as, where possible, private showers, changing areas, and toilet facilities within locker rooms, or separate changing areas, toilets, or showers.[55]

The problem for transgender teens who want to take part in sports is that many school systems have not yet caught up with this ideal situation of providing them with adequate privacy. For financial or other reasons, numerous American school sports programs do not yet properly accommodate trans teens' needs. As a result, a number of young transgender individuals either drop out of those programs or do not join them in the first place.

One example is a trans high school student who was born anatomically a female but identifies as a male. The main reason he has not been able to join his school swimming team is that he still has breasts. That makes it "difficult for me to play sports," he

44

In 2016 demonstrators protest a North Carolina law that bans people from using public bathrooms that align with their gender identity. People have expressed strong feelings about this issue.

says. "I want to be treated as a man, but I can't swim without a top or change in the men's room like a regular guy. This has put me off sports for years, even though I'd love to take part in it."[56]

Controversy over Public Bathrooms

Another tricky and at times controversial issue concerning public accommodations for transgender people is their use of public toilets. In 2015 and 2016, beginning with Mississippi and North Carolina, a number of US states passed laws banning trans people from using bathrooms that align with their gender identity. The proponents of these laws say they are motivated by two general ideas. The first is their belief that even if a man dresses as a woman and calls himself a woman, he is still a male, and males should not be allowed in women's toilet facilities. Second, they worry that male pedophiles, or child molesters, will disguise themselves as women and sexually assault women and children in those facilities.

But many organizations and individuals disagree, among them the American Civil Liberties Union and the Human Rights Campaign. No evidence has been found, they say, of such attacks or other threats posed by transgender people using public bathrooms. The bathroom laws in question are therefore illogical and unreasonable.

Furthermore, some trans individuals have reported that the new anti-transgender bathroom laws promote conflict—and worse. They say that when they merely tried to adhere to these statutes, they encountered mean-spirited confrontation and even violence. One such complaint came from female-to-male transgender teen Payton McGarry. The law in his state dictated that he should use women's public bathrooms because he was born female. So he dutifully did just that, but that led only to trouble. "In high school," McGarry recalls, "as my body started masculinizing, I would walk into a female bathroom and I would be screamed at. I would be pushed and shoved and even slapped. I do not look female. I do not belong in that bathroom."[57]

> "I would walk into a female bathroom and I would be screamed at. I would be pushed and shoved and even slapped."[57]
>
> —Transgender teen Payton McGarry

Similar complaints have been made concerning the use of women's bathrooms by male-to-female trans people. Protesting the North Carolina anti-trans bathroom bill, in 2016 noted photographer Meg Bitton snapped a picture of the young, strikingly feminine and beautiful transgender teen Corey Maison. Bitton posted the photo on Facebook and other popular social media websites. Accompanying the image was a bit of text that read, "If this was *your* daughter, would you be comfortable sending her into a men's bathroom? Neither would I. Be fair. Be kind. Be empathetic. Treat others how you would like to be treated."[58] The photo and the message of the text reportedly changed the minds of a number of the bathroom law's former supporters.

Trying to Be Normal

Belinda was born as a biological, or anatomical, male but identifies herself as a female. One way she has been able to cope with her gender dysphoria, with which she has suffered since childhood, is through frequent cross-dressing in women's clothes. She explains:

> I am a forty-two-year-old who has been cross-dressing at different times since I was a young teenager. I remember wearing my mother's clothes while [going to] school. Both Mom and Dad worked and I was an only child. Every afternoon I would come home from school and try on my mother's clothes.
>
> It felt so wonderful but I was always worried about getting caught by my parents. I remember one Saturday night when they went out and I stayed home. As usual I changed into Mom's clothes and a little bit of make-up. Naturally, I did not have a wig at that stage. They came back about an hour later to collect something Mom needed.
>
> That was the excuse but I now think they suspected something. Anyway, I would not let them in until I changed which took about fifteen minutes. The dressing was hard to explain.
>
> I don't really know why I started cross-dressing but I cannot stop as it gives me so much pleasure. I am a loner who has not had many girlfriends although I have been married once. I think that was just to try to "be normal," however that did not work as I also started wearing my wife's clothes.

Belinda, "Expressing My Feminine Side: Belinda's Personal Story," Gender Centre, October 2013. www .gendercentre.org.au.

Is Being Transgender a Choice?

The issues of playing school sports and using the bathrooms that fit their gender identities are ongoing challenges that trans people face in their everyday lives. In all fairness, they say, they should not have to deal with such challenges. They feel that these are restraints forced on them by cisgender people who do not understand what transgenderism and gender dysphoria are all about.

Unemployment Is High in Transgender Population

Studies show that unemployment rates among transgender individuals are much higher than for other members of the general public. And when unemployment rates are broken out by race and ethnicity, statistics show that transgender people of all backgrounds experience higher unemployment rates than their non-transgender counterparts.

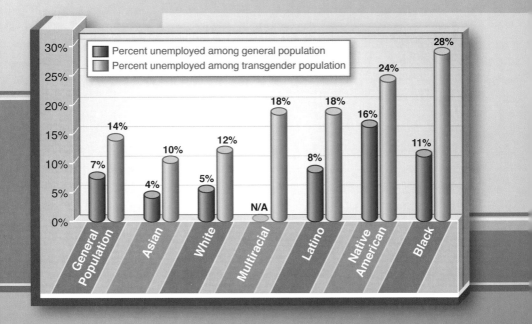

Source: *San Diego Free Press*, "LGBT Economic Empowerment in the Era of Climate Crisis," May 8, 2015. www.sandiegofreepress.org.

Trans people generally see these challenges as attempts to discriminate against them. A directly related issue is the common charge made by cisgender individuals and groups that those who claim to be trans are simply ordinary people looking for special treatment. They have chosen to look and act like members of the opposite gender, according to this view. Supposedly trans people do this because they like to be the center of attention or have some other selfish reason for "pretending" to have a condition called gender dysphoria.

Scientist and medical doctor Danielle Kaufman, who is a male-to-female trans person, strongly refutes that being transgender is a choice. "Gender dysphoria is unspeakably painful," she says, "and changing gender expression is extremely hard. It really would have been a lot easier to have just been born a woman in the first place than to switch." In fact, she continues,

> no one would ever do this unless they were forced to by their own psychology. I did choose to follow a number of specific steps to change my gender expression [i.e., to look like a woman]. It's just that I was so compelled by inner need that I would say it's not really a *choice*. This is so hard that no one would do this if they had any other option. My only other option was to die. And yes, I was prepared to die. I had carefully detailed plans and all the necessary supplies. All I needed were 10 minutes before I went to bed and I wouldn't wake up the next day. I saw it less as suicide and more like euthanasia [mercy killing]. I had a medical condition [gender dysphoria] that bordered on unbearable at times.[59]

What Is It Like to Have Gender Dysphoria?

If being transgender is not a choice, then trans people are markedly different, emotionally and otherwise, from the cisgender individuals who occupy the so-called societal norm. Based on that supposition, it is only natural for cisgender individuals to ask their transgender counterparts how it feels to be themselves. That is, what is it like to live with the gender dysphoria that often develops from being transgender? Put another way, what does it feel like to be part of a small group of individuals whose gender identity and roles do not match up with expected social norms?

One outspoken trans person answers that question with an apt and moving analogy that imagines a person being in a production of one of history's most famous plays. "You are meant to play Romeo," she says. Moreover, the person has gone through all the rehearsals as Romeo right up till the day of the first public performance.

But when opening night comes, the director hands you the script for Juliet. You haven't played this part before, you don't know the lines, the costume doesn't fit at all, and you feel no connection to this character whatsoever. You don't understand what her motivations are, and the director can't explain them in a way that makes any sense to you. But there is no choice. You MUST play Juliet or else everyone will mock you, beat you up, and torment you for years. If you resist, or mess up your lines because they are so foreign to your way of thinking, problem solving or speaking, then you have many weird glances, shoves, stolen textbooks, harassment and insults from your peers to look forward to. It doesn't matter that the role of Romeo is what you truly were born to play. [Like it or not, you must] smile and pretend to enjoy being Juliet. This is what it's like every single day for someone like myself.[60]

CHAPTER FOUR

Can Gender Dysphoria Be Treated or Cured?

Transgenderism is not a disease or mental disorder, but rather a natural deviation within the broad spectrum of human sexuality. Thus, it has no cure—searching for one would be like seeking a cure for being left-handed or having blue eyes.

In contrast, gender dysphoria is a bona fide disorder that causes its sufferers much confusion and mental anguish. No complete cure yet exists for it, but it can be treated in a variety of ways. Before gender dysphoria was recognized as a disorder by international mental health authorities in 2012, doctors tried to treat transgenderism itself. They followed treatment guidelines that evolved over several decades of dealing with trans patients.

When experts finally realized that the problem was gender dysphoria—not simply being transgender—it became necessary to draw up new treatment guidelines. England's Royal College of Psychiatrists led the way, issuing its guidelines in October 2013. First, the document states, people with gender dysphoria have the right to high-quality medical care just like individuals with other mental disorders.

Also, treatment should be multidisciplinary in its approach—that is, the patient should be able to see experts from several different medical disciplines. Further, one of those areas should be psychotherapy, or psychological counseling. Another guideline states that treatment should be tailored to the needs of each individual patient. In addition specific treatments for children and adolescents should continue right into adulthood. In 2015 the American Psychological Association adopted similar guidelines for treating individuals suffering from gender dysphoria.

The wide range of treatments these and other medical authorities recommend include both mental and physical approaches. In addition to psychotherapy, much is currently being done in the area of pharmacologic treatments—those involving various drugs designed to change the way the body develops. In addition to both psychological and drug therapies, some patients turn to a more extreme and permanent approach—surgery, in this case known as sexual reassignment surgery (SRS).

Liberating Years of Pent-Up Emotions

Usually the first step in treating gender dysphoria is some form of psychotherapy. One of these involves the patient seeing a therapist in a series of one-on-one sessions. For teens and even younger patients there is also family therapy, in which the parents talk to the therapist, either with or without the patient present. Group meetings, in which the patient meets with other gender dysphoria sufferers, are also helpful.

Psychotherapy usually involves simply talking, with the therapist both asking and answering questions. Sometimes, however, these discussions are supplemented by alternative sessions. In them, the patients, including transgender children or adolescents, express themselves through drawing, painting, playing music, or performing dances or dramatic skits.

> "Teenagers are generally impatient with their parents' ignorance, doubts, and lack of instantaneous support for gender transition."[61]
>
> —Irwin Krieger, specialist in transgender counseling

Whichever approach is employed, the counselor attempts to get the patient to express and discuss his or her inner feelings. In one-on-one sessions especially, this process can be very emotional. Indeed, many patients, particularly younger ones, have never told anyone about feeling that they are either a male or female trapped in the wrong body. So merely releasing years of pent-up worry, confusion, or even fear and rage can be very liberating.

Cases of teens and children suffering from gender dysphoria also benefit from meetings between the therapist and parents.

Although transgenderism is not considered to be a mental disorder, gender dysphoria is. Experts recommend that treatment, including psychotherapy or other counseling, begin early and continue into adulthood.

Irwin Krieger, who specializes in transgender counseling in New Haven, Connecticut, strongly advocates including parents in the treatment process. "Teenagers are generally impatient with their parents' ignorance, doubts, and lack of instantaneous support for gender transition," he states. He adds that he encourages teens to take some time to fully understand themselves, and

> above all to be patient with their parents and willing to collaborate with them. Teenagers and most young adults realize that the process of transitioning will go better for them in the long run if they have their parents' support. I often point out that simply by being willing to enter into discussion and participate in therapy their parents are offering much more than many teens are able to get from their families.[61]

Medicare Agrees to Pay for SRS

One obstacle that many transgender people seeking sexual reassignment surgery (SRS) have encountered over the years is the high cost of such procedures. Up until 2014 most insurance providers, including Medicare, the US government's medical insurance for people sixty-five and older, refused to pay for such procedures. But in May of that year, this situation changed as the government lifted its ban on Medicare coverage for SRS. This was widely seen as a major victory for transgender rights. Moreover, experts on medical insurance predict that over time this move by Medicare may well pressure some other major insurers to provide similar coverage.

Medicare's long-standing ban on sexual reassignment surgery began in 1981, when such operations were viewed as experimental. But in the decades that followed, all major US medical groups, including the American Medical Association and the American Psychological Association, came to see such surgeries as needed, proper, and safe. Overwhelming evidence had shown that those procedures significantly help people suffering from gender dysphoria. Indeed, while announcing the policy shift, spokespersons for Medicare stated that medical studies conducted over the course of three decades indicated that denying transgender individuals insurance coverage for SRS is unreasonable. "This is long overdue," comments Judith Bradford, of Boston's Fenway Institute, a research facility that deals with health issues affecting transgender and gay people. "It brings government policy in line with the science around trans people's healthcare needs."

Ariana Eunjung Cha, "Ban Lifted on Medicare Coverage for Sex Change Surgery," *Washington Post*, May 30, 2014. www.washingtonpost.com.

The Next Step: Hormone Therapy

Working with a counselor is more often than not quite effective at helping the patient understand why he or she is transgender and has acquired gender dysphoria. Psychotherapy is also valuable in helping patients decide what further steps to take and methods to use in treating their gender dysphoria. However, medical authorities acknowledge that psychotherapy alone is not usually enough to successfully treat gender dysphoria.

Therefore, most patients move on to the next step of treatment. Typically this consists of beginning to transition from the biological gender the patient was born with to the neurological, or brain-centered, gender that the person strongly identifies with. In other words, a patient born a boy will start to transition into a female, while a patient born a girl will begin transitioning into a male. Not all trans people choose to take this step, but the majority does.

Crucial to making such a transition work is drug therapy, in the form of hormone treatments. Two general approaches to hormone therapy for gender dysphoria sufferers are presently in use. One can be used on people of any age. Its goal is to reorient a person's physical attributes to make him or her look like those of a person of the gender opposite his or her anatomical gender. Dr. Mary Harding, an expert on gender transitioning, explains:

> "When people wish to change gender, treatment is given to stop the production of their own hormones, and replace them with the type of hormones they want."[62]
>
> —Dr. Mary Harding, expert on gender transitioning

> When people wish to change gender, treatment is given to stop the production of their own hormones, and replace them with the type of hormones they want. So males who wish to become females . . . are given female hormones (estrogen). The effects of this include bigger breasts, hips and bottoms and prevention of erections. If females wish to become males, [they] are given a male hormone called testosterone. This causes a deeper voice, an enlarged clitoris, and more body hair. It also stops [monthly] periods, and breasts become smaller. Some fat becomes muscle.[62]

Sara's Support System

Although the hormones are usually very effective in making someone look like a member of the opposite gender, this treatment will be more successful from a mental health standpoint if the patient can lean on a support system during the transition. It significantly helps if relatives, friends, and even coworkers show understanding and give the patient positive feedback. That way, his or her mental attitude will be equally positive while undergoing this major physical change.

One male-to-female trans woman named Sara was fortunate enough to have such a support system in place when she underwent hormone therapy. After the hormones started to take effect and make her former male self "present as," or look, more female, a close friend told her, "You make sense now."[63] Clearly, those who knew Sara before treatment began always felt that she did not seem to fit comfortably in a male persona. Now that she was blossoming into a young woman, her outward appearance finally seemed to jibe with the female personality she had displayed all along.

Sara was lucky enough to receive similar positive feedback and support from her coworkers. Even her workplace, where she had been employed for only about six months when she came out, was completely accepting. She recalls, "I was presenting as Sara everywhere except work, and because of the hormones I'd started having to bind myself," or use a stretchy piece of material to press on and flatten her breasts. Sara felt she had to do this because at work she presented as her original male self and was used to getting up each "morning and putting on a suit and tie." But this changed when she told the company's human resources director the truth. "I was a transgender woman," she blurted out, "and had been presenting as Sara everywhere but work."[64]

The woman to whom Sara made her brave and heartfelt admission reacted no less positively than the young woman's family and friends had. "She was amazing," Sara recollects. "She said she'd do whatever was needed to make it work for me. When I told my direct boss, his response was, 'Oh, thank God! I thought you were going to tell me you were quitting!'"[65] Her boss also went along with Sara's proposed way of formally coming out to her regular coworkers. She penned a letter to everyone in the company, telling them she was transgender and what that meant. On a Friday afternoon, she distributed the letter and left work as the man they had long known. The following Monday she returned to work as Sara and enjoyed a warm welcome from all.

Hormone Blockers Provide Extra Time

Sara underwent hormone therapy because she was an adult who had already made up her mind about what to do about her gender identity—she was certain she wanted to transition from a male into a female. The other general approach to employing hormones to treat gender dysphoria is used almost strictly with younger patients—most often in their early teens. Young people in this age group may not yet understand enough about their condition to make a rational decision about whether or not to undergo transition, or they might simply need a bit more time to think it through and discuss it with their parents.

In the meantime, these young people know they are about to experience puberty—when their bodies will go through the natural maturing process from child to young adult. In the years before reaching puberty, they may have felt they could tough out the confusion and misery caused by their dysphoria. But reaching puberty almost always makes these negative feelings even worse. "Children who identify as male may begin to develop breasts," one researcher explains, "or those who identify as female may start growing facial hair." For those children who undergo such changes, "confusion and depression often follow puberty's onset. Studies show that more than half of transgender youth have attempted suicide at least once before their twentieth birthday."[66]

To give these young people breathing space to decide on a direction, doctors will often prescribe so-called hormone blockers. Used in the right manner and correct dosage, such drugs will temporarily block, or postpone, the onset of puberty. "With hormone blockers—drugs that have safely been used in other contexts for a very long time—we can hit the 'pause' button on puberty,"[67] remarks gender identity specialist Dr. Johanna Olson of Children's Hospital in Los Angeles.

> "With hormone blockers . . . we can hit the 'pause' button on puberty."[67]
>
> —Dr. Johanna Olson, gender identity specialist

The use of hormone blockers has several major advantages. First, the trans youth has extra time to educate him- or herself, if he or she has not already done so, and consider the available options. Also, the young person's parents may have needed time to absorb the shock and overcome the confusion they often feel on learning their child is transgender. Frequently, using hormone blockers buys precious time in which parents more often than not gain understanding about their son's or daughter's plight and in the long run provide him or her with unconditional support.

Finally, hormone blockers are easily reversible. If the patient and his or her parents agree that they do not desire the full transition to take place, the doctor can withdraw the blockers. After that, the patient's body will undergo puberty in a natural way and in fairly short order.

Preparing for Surgery

Some trans people who go through a successful transition using hormone therapy feel that they need no further treatment. That means they do not take the final potential step in treatment for gender dysphoria—sexual reassignment surgery (SRS). In such cases, male-to-female trans individuals will retain their male genitals even though they will thereafter dress and behave as women. Conversely, some female-to-male trans people, often referred to as FTMs (the abbreviated form of "female to male"), will dress and live as men yet retain their vaginas.

Although these people never totally transition physically, for one reason or another they feel they do not need to. One FTM, who goes by the name JohnnyMac online, says, "I've been taking testosterone shots for about three years now. But I haven't had surgery as yet." He feels he does not need SRS because he already passes "as male pretty much unequivocally [undeniably]; I have a goatee, and that certainly tips the balance in my favor." He adds, "I might just keep my vagina."[68]

Those trans individuals who do choose to move on to SRS usually cannot do so immediately. This is because most members of the medical community have erected a sort of safeguard that purposely slows down the final phase of the transition process.

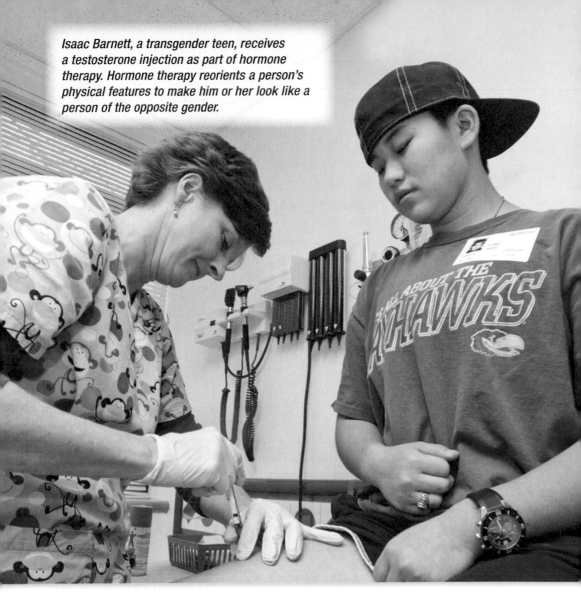

Isaac Barnett, a transgender teen, receives a testosterone injection as part of hormone therapy. Hormone therapy reorients a person's physical features to make him or her look like a person of the opposite gender.

Before reassignment surgery, most doctors and clinics that treat gender dysphoria now recommend that their patients go through a trial period sometimes called "Real Life Experience," or RLE for short.

RLE consists of a period of time in which a trans person lives twenty-four hours a day for several months in the gender with which her or his brain identifies. That includes wearing the clothes associated with that preferred gender and no longer hiding in the proverbial closet. Thus, if the surgical candidate has not yet come out to family, friends, or the public in general, he or she must do so during the RLE. According to a spokesperson for a clinic that does sexual reassignment surgery and requires a period of RLE,

> People have fewer regrets after hormones and surgery if they have had experience living full time in their preferred gender. In addition, there are some people who, having been very clear that they wanted surgery at the outset, decide even as late as 18 months [into the process] that they do not want these interventions.[69]

Several Surgical Options

If the patient gets through the Real Life Experience and feels confident about going forward with the surgery, the next step is to decide which kind of operation she or he will have. A number of different surgical options are presently open to trans people who are transitioning. One involves altering the genitals of a male who wants to transition to a female. Doctors remove the existing penis and testicles. In their place, employing the latest plastic surgery techniques, they fashion female genitals, including a vaginal opening, labia, and clitoris.

In the opposite case—that of a woman who wants to transition into a man—the surgeons begin by removing the uterus. Depending on the situation, they may or may not also take out the ovaries and fallopian tubes—the tubes that connect the ovaries to the uterus. Then the doctors create a penis, testicles, and scrotum (the sac containing the testicles), using skin taken from the inner arm or lower section of the abdomen. Sometimes the surgeons instead leave the clitoris in place and employ hormones to enlarge it into an organ that resembles a small penis.

Usually, female-to-male trans people opting for surgery also have their breasts removed in a procedure called a mastectomy. This surgery is often done separately from the one that deals with the genital area. In contrast, males who are transitioning into females often undergo surgery to enlarge their breasts.

Although these four procedures are the most common gender-transition surgeries, they are by no means the only ones. Some patients also opt for facial plastic surgery. For instance, a

Trying to Make Oneself Feel Better

The difficulties of living with gender dysphoria can sometimes make a trans person feel that life is hopeless, says Sarah Karlan, a reporter and editor for BuzzFeed News. Karlan has collected snippets of advice from many transgender people she has interviewed. They all told her what they like to do to make themselves feel better. Some of their replies include:

"When my dysphoria gets bad, I take out my guitar and play music. Sometimes I like to play *my* own music, music I wrote. Mostly I just cover songs. When I play, I feel like I'm in my own world, just my mind, my hands and my guitar."

"Usually I get through my bad days by trying to talk slower and quieter, as that usually makes my voice sound a little deeper. I usually let my mind drift off to my favorite playlists or maybe try to talk to friends."

"I like to get as cold as I impossibly can (open a window, take off all my clothes) and get into a really hot shower or bath and wash away the cold."

"I've found that good nutrition and exercise has helped tremendously. My mood is better, I feel healthier, and it's something I never really believed I could do, but now I know I can."

"If you've been feeling really dysphoric for a while, spend a day dressed as your stereotypical biological sex. You'll feel awful for the day, but the day after when you dress as your actual gender will be awesome."

Quoted in Sarah Karlan, "20 Small Things to Do When Gender Dysphoria Gets You Down," BuzzFeed LGBT, December 6, 2015. www.buzzfeed.com.

male transitioning into a female may desire to make his face look more feminine.

Voice surgery is still another option. "Hormone treatment can cause a deeper voice for females becoming male," Dr. Harding explains. "However, for men to have a higher-pitched, female-sounding voice, they may need voice therapy or an operation."[70] In addition, minor cosmetic procedures often aid trans women in transitioning. These include removing unwanted body hair using electrolysis or lasers or undergoing hair transplants to create a fuller head of hair.

Sam Moehlig's Story

Many adult trans people have undergone these surgical procedures. A number of teenagers have done so as well, although sexual reassignment surgery for individuals younger than eighteen remains controversial. In fact, several surgeons refuse to do such operations. Most often they argue that legal minors are not mature enough to make an informed decision on something so important and life altering. A number of hospitals also oppose SRS for younger teens. Rady Children's Hospital in San Diego, for example, is only one of several children's hospitals that will not perform sexual reassignment surgery on teenagers younger than sixteen.

Some hospitals will perform SRS on younger teens in cases in which the patient's parents strongly support that avenue of treatment. One such case was that of a female-to-male trans person named Sam Moehlig, who had the surgery at age fourteen. Named Samantha by his parents at birth, this Southern California native endured years of mental torment and suffered almost constantly from severe clinical depression. Moreover, he was so miserable living as a girl that he frequently had suicidal thoughts.

Samantha's frantic parents, Kathie and Ron, wisely turned to professional counseling for their troubled daughter. The months of psychotherapy that followed confirmed what Samantha had long insisted to her parents and other relatives—that she was a boy trapped in a girl's body. The psychiatrist gave the distraught family a clinical term to describe the girl's condition—gender dysphoria. Surgeons the family consulted agreed. The unanimous diagnosis was that Samantha was transgender and undergoing a particularly harsh onslaught of mental distress over it.

The child then went through many more months of counseling, during which she adopted a male persona and name—Sam. Eventually, all of the parties involved agreed they should move on to the next logical step—hormone blockers. Sam had testosterone shots and soon began outwardly to look like a boy. Fortunately for him, he was homeschooled, which meant that he did not have to deal with cruel taunts and other abuses from classmates.

Sam felt that one problem remained, namely his breasts, which he saw as potent symbols of his original female self. His parents came to agree that removing them would help a great deal in his transition from Samantha to Sam. "I was finally getting rid of something that had been bothering me for years," the fourteen-year-old Sam remarked. The surgery was a success. Not long afterward, the young man said, "I am grateful I was born the way I was. I look back on it," and without this experience, "I don't think I would be the type of person I am."[71] His father was also upbeat about the series of treatments that had transformed his daughter into a son. The elder Moehlig listed the benefits the young man had gained: "His own comfort. The way he'll be accepted. Not having to hide anything. The barriers are down. He can do whatever he wants to do, be whatever he wants to be, and do it from his authentic self."[72]

An Astounding Success Rate

It turns out that Sam Moehlig is not alone in his satisfaction with the series of medical approaches he underwent to treat his gender dysphoria. Indeed, the vast majority of transgender people who complete a full transition to their preferred gender identity end up happy and well-adjusted. This fact is confirmed by numerous studies: A review of most of those conducted between 1996 and 2016 found that an astounding 96 percent of the trans individuals who had comprehensive treatment, including SRS, were fully satisfied with the results.

> "Every person is different. That's who I am."[73]
>
> —Sam Moehlig, former gender dysphoria patient

An estimated ninety thousand Americans have thus far undergone such full transitions from one gender to the other. They will always remain transgender people, to be sure. But they no longer suffer from the anguish of gender dysphoria, and they are proud to be who, in their minds, they were always supposed to be. It may be that the courageous young Sam Moehlig spoke for all of them when he said, "Every person is different. That's who I am."[73]

SOURCE NOTES

Introduction: "God Made a Mistake"

1. Quoted in Hanna Rosin, "A Boy's Life," *Atlantic,* November 2008. www.theatlantic.com.
2. Quoted in Rosin, "A Boy's Life."
3. Quoted in Rosin, "A Boy's Life."
4. Quoted in Rosin, "A Boy's Life."
5. Quoted in Rosin, "A Boy's Life."
6. Quoted in Rosin, "A Boy's Life."
7. Quoted in Trey Sanchez, "CBS Runs Story on Transgender Children," June 9, 2014. www.truthrevolt.org.
8. Quoted in Kids in the House, "Issues Facing a Gender Non-Comforming Child." www.kidsinthehouse.com.

Chapter One: What Is Gender Dysphoria?

9. Quoted in Amy Lynn Smith, "Hunter's Story: Flourishing in an Affirming Environment," *Eclectablog* (blog), May 9, 2016. www.eclectablog.com.
10. Quoted in Smith, "Hunter's Story."
11. Benjamin C. Harris, "Likely Transgender Individuals in U.S. Federal Administrative Records and the 2010 Census," US Census Bureau, May 2016. www.census.gov.
12. Quoted in Smith, "Hunter's Story."
13. Quoted in Smith, "Hunter's Story."
14. Quoted in Amy Lynn Smith, "Reid's Story: Speaking Out for Safe Spaces," *Eclectablog* (blog), May 26, 2016. www.eclectablog.com.
15. Quoted in Smith, "Reid's Story."
16. Mohammed A. Memon, "Gender Dysphoria and Transgenderism: Background," Medscape, February 2016. http://e medicine.medscape.com.
17. Mayo Clinic, "Depression: What Does the Term 'Clinical Depression' Mean?" www.mayoclinic.org.

18. Quoted in Amy Lynn Smith, "Jay's Story: Falling in Love with Himself," *Eclectablog* (blog), April 18, 2016. www.eclecta blog.com.
19. Quoted in Smith, "Jay's Story."
20. Quoted in Smith, "Jay's Story."
21. Quoted in Amy Lynn Smith, "Coleen's Story: Unconditional Love and Support," *Eclectablog* (blog), April 6, 2016. www .eclectablog.com.
22. Christabel Edwards, "Gendered Toys: A Transgender Perspective," *Let Toys Be Toys* (blog), December 6, 2013. www .lettoysbetoys.org.uk.
23. Edwards, "Gendered Toys."

Chapter Two: What Causes Gender Dysphoria?

24. Zack Ford, "APA Revises Manual: Being Transgender Is No Longer a Mental Disorder," ThinkProgress, December 2, 2012. http://thinkprogress.org.
25. Lynn Conway, "Basic TG/TS/IS Information." http://ai.eecs. umich.edu/people/conway/TS/TS.html.
26. Conway, "Basic TG/TS/IS Information."
27. Conway, "Basic TG/TS/IS Information."
28. Quoted in Amy Lynn Smith, "Jayne's Story: Revealing the Woman Within," *Eclectablog* (blog), May 17, 2016. www .eclectablog.com.
29. Quoted in Smith, "Jayne's Story."
30. Quoted in Smith, "Jayne's Story."
31. Gender Centre, "Surviving as an Effeminate Child in an Extremely Homophobic Family," September 2013. www.gender centre.org.au.
32. Gender Centre, "Surviving as an Effeminate Child in an Extremely Homophobic Family."
33. Ananya Mandal, "Causes of Gender Dysphoria," December 2013. www.news-medical.net.
34. Conway, "Basic TG/TS/IS Information."
35. Conway, "Basic TG/TS/IS Information."
36. Conway, "Basic TG/TS/IS Information."

37. Transas City, "The Transgender Brain." http://transascity.org.
38. L. Fleming Fallon, "Gender Identity Disorder," Encyclopedia of Mental Disorders. www.minddisorders.com.
39. Conway, "Basic TG/TS/IS Information."
40. Conway, "Basic TG/TS/IS Information."
41. Conway, "Basic TG/TS/IS Information."
42. Quoted in Amy Lynn Smith, "Char's Story: Visibility, Lost and Found," *Eclectablog* (blog), March 31, 2016. www.eclecta blog.com.

Chapter Three: What Is It Like to Live with Gender Dysphoria?

43. Conway, "Basic TG/TS/IS Information."
44. Sophia Gubb, "What It Feels Like to Be Transgender (and Why Trans Genders Are Valid)," August 23, 2013. www.sophia gubb.com.
45. *Tarnished Sophia* (blog), "Wrong Body, Right Mind: Living with Gender Dysphoria," June 16, 2013. https://tarnishedsophia. wordpress.com.
46. *Tarnished Sophia* (blog), "Wrong Body, Right Mind."
47. Marika K. Jackson, "My Struggle with Identity," Gender Centre, October 2013. www.gendercentre.org.au.
48. Jackson, "My Struggle with Identity."
49. Jackson, "My Struggle with Identity."
50. Anonymous, "Eloqui: No Longer a Shroud of Clouded Roles," Gender Centre, October 2013. www.gendercentre.org.au.
51. Janet E. Fletcher, "Why We Lie: And We Lie to the Most Important People in Our Lives," Gender Centre, October 2013. www.gendercentre.org.au.
52. Jackson, "My Struggle with Identity."
53. Fletcher, "Why We Lie."
54. Women's Sports Foundation, "Participation of Transgender Athletes in Women's Sports." www.womenssportsfoundation .org.
55. Women's Sports Foundation, "Participation of Transgender Athletes in Women's Sports."

56. Maximilian Roele, "Living with Gender Dysphoria," *Leiden Psychology Blog,* June 9, 2015. www.leidenpsychologyblog.nl.

57. Quoted in Alia E. Dastagir, "The Imaginary Predator in America's Transgender Bathroom War," *USA Today,* April 29, 2016. www.usatoday.com.

58. Quoted in Almie Rose, "Photo Shoot of Transgender Girl Sparks Debate About Bathroom Bills and Beauty," ATTN:, April 27, 2016. www.attn.com.

59. Danielle Kaufman, "The Dark Side of Being Transgender: Having Little Choice," *Huffington Post,* February 2, 2016. www.huffingtonpost.com.

60. *Tarnished Sophia* (blog), "Wrong Body, Right Mind."

Chapter Four: Can Gender Dysphoria Be Treated or Cured?

61. Irwin Krieger, "Authenticity and Safety: Family Therapy with Transgender Teens," *Social Work Today*, www.socialworktoday.com.

62. Mary Harding, "Gender Dysphoria," Patient. http://patient.info.

63. Quoted in Amy Lynn Smith, "Sara's Story: Finding Her Place in the World," *Eclectablog* (blog), May 25, 2016. www.eclectablog.com.

64. Quoted in Smith, "Sara's Story."

65. Quoted in Smith, "Sara's Story."

66. Christopher Wanjek, "Pausing Puberty with Hormone Blockers May Help Transgender Kids," Live Science, May 6, 2016. www.livescience.com.

67. Quoted in Wanjek, "Pausing Puberty with Hormone Blockers May Help Transgender Kids."

68. Quoted in The Straight Dope, "Ask the Transsexual." http://boards.straightdope.com.

69. Nottingham Centre for Gender Dysphoria, "Frequently Asked Questions." www.nottinghamshirehealthcare.nhs.uk.

70. Harding, "Gender Dysphoria."

71. Quoted in Peter Rowe, "How a Girl Born at Two Pounds Became a Happy Boy," *San Diego Union-Tribune*, April 7, 2016. www.sandiegouniontribune.com.
72. Quoted in Rowe, "How a Girl Born at Two Pounds Became a Happy Boy."
73. Quoted in Rowe, "How a Girl Born at Two Pounds Became a Happy Boy."

RECOGNIZING SIGNS OF TROUBLE

According to the US National Library of Medicine, the symptoms of gender dysphoria are not the same for everyone. Age and social environment may influence symptoms.

Children may:
• Be disgusted by their own genitals
• Be rejected by their peers; feel alone
• Believe that they will grow up to become the opposite sex
• Say that they want to be the opposite sex

Adults may:
• Dress like the opposite sex
• Feel alone
• Want to live as a person of the opposite sex
• Wish to be rid of their own genitals

Adults and children may:
• Cross-dress; show habits typical of the opposite sex
• Have depression or anxiety
• Withdraw from social interaction

US National Library of Medicine, "Gender Dysphoria," MedlinePlus. https://medlineplus.gov.

The following organizations offer information and support for teens and others who are transgender, and help for those who are suffering from gender dysphoria.

Human Rights Campaign (HRC)

1640 Rhode Island Ave. NW
Washington, DC 20036
website: www.hrc.org

HRC provides a national voice on gay, lesbian, bisexual, and transgender issues. The group lobbies Congress and promotes community education projects relating to transgender people.

International Foundation for
Gender Education (IFGE)

PO Box 540229
Waltham, MA 02454
website: www.ifge.org

IFGE provides information about psychotherapy, counseling, and support groups that help transgender people, in the form of books, magazines, and videos.

National Center for Transgender
Equality (NCTE)

1325 Massachusetts Ave., Suite 700
Washington, DC 20005
website: http://transequality.org

NCTE is an organization dedicated to helping transgender people achieve social justice and equality, in part by educating members of Congress about transgender issues and needs.

PFLAG (formerly known as Parents, Families and Friends of Lesbians and Gays)
1828 L St., Suite 660
Washington, DC 20036
website: www.pflag.org

PFLAG's mission is to promote the interests and well-being of lesbian, bisexual, gay, and transgender Americans wherever and whenever possible.

Transgender Law Center
1629 Telegraph Ave., Suite 400
Oakland, CA 94612
website: http://transgenderlawcenter.org

The Transgender Law Center tries to alter laws and attitudes relating to transgender people and issues in hopes that all Americans can express themselves the way they choose and live together in harmony.

Transgender Legal Defense and Education Fund
20 W. 20th St., Suite 705
New York, NY 10011
website: www.transgenderlegal.org

The Transgender Legal Defense and Education Fund works hard to end discrimination based upon gender identity and to bring about equality for transgender people in society.

Trans Youth Equality Foundation
PO Box 7441
Portland, ME 04112
website: www.transyouthequality.org

The Trans Youth Equality Foundation provides educational material and other support for transgender children and teens and their families.

FOR FURTHER RESEARCH

Books

Lisa Alexandra, *Becoming Lisa: A Transgender Journey.* Washington, DC: Amazon Digital Services, 2016.

Arin Andrews, *Some Assembly Required: The Not-So-Secret Life of a Transgender Teen.* New York: Simon & Schuster, 2015.

Kenna Dixon, *I'm Not the Man I Used to Be.* Los Gatos, CA: Smashwords, 2014.

Jazz Jennings, *Being Jazz: My Life as a Transgender Teen.* New York: Crown, 2016.

Susan Kuklin, *Beyond Magenta: Transgender Teens Speak Out.* London: Walker, 2016.

Julia Medsker, *Coming to Life: One Mother's Journey with Her Transgender Daughter.* Washington, DC: Amazon Digital Services, 2016.

Rylan J. Testa, Deborah Coolhart, and Jayme Peta, *The Gender Quest Workbook: A Guide to Teens & Young Adults Exploring Gender Identity.* Oakland, CA: Instant Help, 2015.

Internet Sources

American Civil Liberties Union, "Transgender Rights." www.aclu.org/issues/lgbt-rights/transgender-rights.

Gender Centre, "Surviving as an Effeminate Child in an Extremely Homophobic Family," September 2013. www.gendercentre.org.au/resources/polare-archive/archived-articles/surviving.htm.

GLAAD, "Transgender FAQ." www.glaad.org/transgender/transfaq.

Emanuella Grinberg, "Transgender Student Accuses School of 'Stigmatizing' Treatment," CNN, July 21, 2016. www.cnn.com/2016/07/20/us/wisconsin-transgender-student-lawsuit.

Emma Margolin, "NBA Pulls All-Star Game Out of Charlotte over Transgender Bathroom Law HB2," NBC Out, July 21, 2016. www.nbcnews.com/feature/nbc-out/nba-pulls-all-star-game-out-charlotte-over-hb2-n614466.

Claire C. Miller, "The Search for the Best Estimate of the Transgender Population," *New York Times,* June 8, 2015. www.nytimes.com/2015/06/09/upshot/the-search-for-the-best-estimate-of-the-transgender-population.html?_r=0.

New York Times Editorial Board, "Transgender Today," May 4, 2015. www.nytimes.com/2015/05/04/opinion/the-quest-for-transgender-equality.html?_r=0.

Matthew Rosenberg, "Transgender People Will Be Allowed to Serve Openly in Military," *New York Times*, June 30, 2016. www.nytimes.com/2016/07/01/us/transgender-military.html.

Hanna Rosin, "A Boy's Life," *Atlantic,* November 2008. www.theatlantic.com/magazine/archive/2008/11/a-boys-life/307059.

Amy Lynn Smith, "Introducing a Story Series About the Lives of Transgender People," *Eclectablog* (blog), March 30, 2016. www.eclectablog.com/2016/03/introducing-a-story-series-about-the-lives-of-transgender-people.html.

US National Library of Medicine, "Gender Dysphoria," MedlinePlus. https://medlineplus.gov/ency/article/001527.htm.

WebMD, "What It Means to Be Transgender." www.webmd.com/a-to-z-guides/features/transgender-what-it-means.

INDEX

PICTURE CREDITS

Cover: Depositphotos/michaeldb

6: Associated Press

10: Maury Aaseng

16: Depositphotos/s_bukley

19: iStockphoto.com/poplasen

25: Thinkstock Images/targovcom

30: Biophoto Associates/Science Source

33: Shutterstock.com/Image Point Fr

38: Maury Aaseng

45: iStockphoto.com/AwakenedEye

48: Maury Aaseng

53: Thinkstock Images/KatarzynaBialasiewicsz

59: Kansas City Star/Tribune News Service

ABOUT THE AUTHOR

In addition to his numerous acclaimed volumes on ancient civilizations, historian Don Nardo has published several studies of modern scientific and medical discoveries and phenomena. They include *Vaccines, Teens and Birth Control, Breast Cancer, The Deadliest Dinosaurs, The Scientific Revolution,* and *Eating Disorders.* Nardo, who also composes and arranges orchestral music, lives with his wife, Christine, in Massachusetts.